LITTLE WISDOMS

Other books by Solee MacIsaac

Joy Shared
A Beloved Speck in the Universe

Little Wisdoms

Solee MacIsaac

EVERY BOOK PRESS
MMXXIII

© Copyright 2023 Solee MacIsaac
All rights reserved.
ISBN: 978-0-9837714-6-3

Cover Photo:
The author's son, Michael Parks, at age four

Book Design:
William Bentley

INTRODUCTION

These small angles of thought were written in May and June of 2022. Spring seems to inspire writing. The process of formulating and composing has helped me to have a stronger focus on what is most important to me. Although not everyone may think these quips wise, here are they humbly presented. Hopefully, open hearts will benefit by reading, and passing them on to others. I do not claim to be able to live up to what is printed here, but I will continue to try.

Solee MacIsaac

This book is dedicated to my son, Michael, who gave me this title, "Little Wisdoms." His constant good nature and loving support continues to hold me up. His little boy laughing face on the cover reminds me that wisdom is often learned with a sense of humor.

Open for heart work,
Happy effort
For those who love.

LITTLE WISDOMS

Don't struggle over "free will,"
Consider what you can change
In this moment.

Laughing uses many muscles;
Crying, few;
Being present, none.

Climbing the ladder to
Success means
Raising your state.

The Golden Rule
Guides all to collect
Inner wealth.

Love engenders
Whirlwind forces spiraling
Positive possibilities.

Don't be afraid of not being loved,
You are blessed
Beyond measure.

Having no love, means
Your circle includes
Only you.

A leap of faith
Is a genuine stretching
Of the soul.

Building a vehicle to cross
The boundary of death
Is miraculous.

Living a true life
Means existing
With open eye.

Truth is
Much larger
Than mere honesty.

Suffering,
Well used,
Creates new being.

Reflection can bring
Remorse
And renewal.

Time does not exist
Outside of
Now.

Beauty is
Wonderful, and
A temptress.

We are small
Beings with
Large dreams.

Breathing the biosphere,
Eating the very Earth,
Seeing reflected spirit.

Life, the true green,
Growing, emerging,
Whole.

Chasing yourself
Around the wheel
Is a fool's pursuit.

The flesh of the Earth
Is a playground
For the uninitiated.

Waking to blessed dawn
Leaves hypnotic
Sleep behind.

Morning birdsong
Cheers a gloomy
Outlook.

If your hair
Isn't on fire,
You haven't seen truth.

Wade through heavy murk,
Reach for the saving rope.
Pull yourself out of despair.

Look up,
Blue, strong, sky space
Beckons.

This dream of life
Recedes with awareness
Of Reality.

Only in the present moment
Can anything,
At all, happen.

Gray hair, gray eyes,
Gray soul: it is time to
Pierce this form.

Reborn to newness,
Allow the flood of color
To awaken baby joy.

Holding your horses
Is better than
Wild riding into chaos.

Intelligent leaders
Are calm
And patient.

Darker moments are
Dispelled with one word:
Be.

Action coupled with
Lighted purpose
Produces positive currents.

Reverse your direction,
Examine motive,
Proceed in a new way.

How does this action
Align with the ultimate
Aim?

Long to touch
The untouchable,
To see the unseeable.

Longing for You,
The inner
Unknowable.

Dense and cluttered,
Mind tool
Needs sharpening.

Relief to need little,
To be simply
Content.

Standing on hilltop,
Realizing all below
That holds me up.

There is no organization
Without
Prioritizing.

All bits of information
Are part of
Something larger.

The way things are connected
Is usually
Beyond our scope.

Movements on a higher
Level can cause
Earthquakes.

Strings holding us
Together
Reverberate harmonically.

Water, magical fluid
Of which we are composed,
Seeps its way.

Let all undecided and not
Understood rest easily
While digesting.

Grapple with the devils
That prompt sleepy
Decisions.

Kneel before
The giver of all
Beneficence.

Gratitude opens
Inner doorways
Reason cannot touch.

Privacy of body shell
Is safety net
Or prison.

Languid and unplugged:
Infancy,
A sprouting seed.

Ancient adages
Give advice,
Drink deep.

Lavender moments,
Past remembrances,
Trail regret and longing.

Quivering hair follicles,
Rainbow eyes,
Scratching underbelly.

Earthly beings teach
What they know
By being what they are.

Strawberry rhubarb pie,
Lattice top,
Gone in thirty seconds.

Memory twists and
Meanders like a river
Lost in the forest.

Radiant light,
Whether Sun or
Explosion, reveals.

Hardening to outside
Influences
Is a lonely dwelling place.

Old man and
His dreams
Sip his tea.

Spend years doing any one thing,
And oddly become good
At many things.

Generous and Kind
Walk together
Holding hands.

Sky is large
And scary,
The top of our bubble.

We are all
Sweet,
In our heart of heart.

From above
We must look crazy
In our pursuits.

Genuine love
Soothes
Heart wounds.

Stretch out your cramped
Inner world,
Feel the light spaces.

Soft and yielding,
Our form is molded
Around empty space.

Nothing, no thing,
Living or dead,
Catches your fire.

Watching where you step
Is more important
Than you think.

To develop wings
Flying must be
In your soul.

Protecting worth
Is a lifelong
Effort.

Grace is
Bestowed on
Worthy beings.

Open your heart
Like a rose
To the sun.

Be alert
At the gate
To utter silence.

Working with joy in your
Heart
Is real accomplishment.

Humble efforts
Proceed with ease
From right understandings.

The entire picture
Cannot be seen
From a single perspective.

A calm center needs no explanation.
We are mere reflections of the grand design;
Animals and plants do a better job.

Resonating with a higher level,
Brilliance appears
That isn't ours.

We are vessels
That know not
How to be filled.

Resting on laurels
We did not earn,
Life continues uninterrupted.

Golden ring seems
Out of reach.
Grow a longer arm.

Formality can focus
Attention on higher values,
Or just be uncomfortable.

Do we love or resent
Our parents, who
Love us anyway.

Hasten to who loves you most,
Let no obstacles
Impede your journey.

Lay flowering boughs
Before the staircase,
Ascend above the sky.

At last, Love has entered,
And taken residence
In open heart.

What is full, is really empty;
What is empty,
Is really lucky.

Tears can cleanse
The pathway to greater
Understanding.

Let no hardship
Be neglected by
Self-pity.

Ever climbing,
Don't miss the destination
Right in front of you.

Round, smooth, and whole,
A water droplet contains
An eternal world.

Light penetrates
Whether we perceive it,
Or not.

All is visible
In lighted
Eternity.

Together we are stronger,
Holding fast the saving rope,
Meeting eye to eye.

Unleash wild ecstasy
Before the open doorway,
Don't hold back.

If you love someone,
Don't punish them
For not being who you are.

Be willing to allow
That you may have
Misunderstood.

Mistakes can teach,
But try to
Not repeat them.

Dimpled pool,
Reflections swirled,
Shoreline golden-eyed.

Behold enormous, golden
Inner space of Presence
Shining from your eyes.

Little known,
We are paupers,
Slowly growing wings.

Disconnected from
Who I think I am,
Confused and heightened.

Beautiful sounds
Enhance a growing
Soul.

Disagreeing
Does not
Preclude loving.

Wise dome,
Eliminating all unnecessary,
Simple and perfect.

Creating a joyous and
Present state,
High endeavor.

Clean and orderly
Go a long way
Toward setting the stage.

To attract higher influences,
Clear your heart
And mind.

Gentle, kind, and loving,
Higher guides
Can seem ferocious.

Lay down your weapons,
Prostrate before
Teachers of Love.

Gathering in name
Of joining Light together,
Magnifies torch held high.

Give your best
To all who adhere
To the loving Light.

Spread before you tools
Ready to secure
Presence.

Leave space for
The third motive
In building, creating, accomplishing.

As actors, all is done
With us,
Or without us.

We have not written this Play,
But sometimes can
Appreciate its magic.

When arriving
Drop all shields,
Absorb every photon.

Burning heart flame
Beaming rays of Light,
Lighter than Light.

Take the Muse
On her terms
When she arrives.

Gather all the love you can
Into your arms,
'Til it implodes in your heart.

Needs may be simple,
But necessary.
Wants come and go.

Messages obscured,
Hidden, indecipherable,
Point to unknowable Self.

A short trip from here to
Here,
Is enjoyable together.

What is simpler
Than
To Be.

Greatness is of the heart,
Not the pocket
Or the abode.

Sofia, Greek wisdom,
Is feminine,
Like God.

Love like you
May see them no more.
Live like the last day of life.

Not everything
Is reasonable
Or knowable.

What is God-like?
We only
Guess.

Wasted, the outpourings
Of a generous heart onto
Barren understandings.

Symbols can convey
More than
Pristine vision.

An egret, alone and white,
Stands in utter stillness
Before a dark green life.

Silent nothing,
Large and luminous,
Overfills small self.

Relatedness connects
Immense distances.
No space, no time, no matter.

What is important?
Realizing position and
Situation, now.

Drink deep
Cold blue truth;
Dispel all erroneous.

Adorned with golden hills and valleys,
Wind-braided hair,
Bride waits in Mother Earth.

Digging for nuggets
Without Presence
Yields fool's gold.

Pure heart, clear mind,
Clean body:
A fruitful pyramid.

Red shocking disruption
Sends glaring light,
Forcing new perspective.

The greater the gift,
The larger the payment:
Keep small and simple.

All is love,
Do not stress over
Helpful medicine.

Always remember
Who you are,
And who you are not.

Living in the mountains,
Seeing your face
Everywhere, even on mine.

Nature's beings reflect
Beauty of their creators,
Love seeks lovers.

Reveal your inner beauty
To all who revere
Highest aims.

Courageous heart
Naively tries
To love all.

Love frequency
Is very high, fine, strong,
And lasting.

When inner light
Is stronger than the Sun,
Harmony reigns.

Kindle heart fire,
Swim in the sacred waters,
Live the unknowing life.

Surmount sorrow,
Climb into clear
Heart-space each moment.

Humility cannot be other
Than our state.
Feel the fluttering wings.

Graceless are those
Who act or speak
In a superior way.

Keys and locks
Are for valuables,
And secrets.

Nothing is secret,
Really,
In Uncreated Light.

Awaken to all the
Joy, love, and light
You have been gifted.

Air, water, light, food, heat –
What is actually a need?
Does beauty play a role?

Learning to appreciate
Finer aspects of life,
Continues until death.

We see, hear,
Feel;
Does it register?

Memory is
Moment
Fixed in amber.

Many moments pass us by,
As we have stopped
In inner tracks.

Kindness is a virtue
Often underestimated,
But greatly appreciated.

We are creatures
With feet in two worlds,
And heads in the clouds.

Pull the rug over your head,
Peek out when light returns,
New day begins well.

It takes more than
Milk and honey
To nourish a flagging soul.

Great art as beautiful
As it can be,
How much more its counterpart.

Archetypes precede
Their reflections
On Earth.

Every opportunity
Begins small and
Expands with attention.

Nothing is really personal
Except
What you hold apart.

Finding your path
Means you have one,
Does it mean you lost it?

Marriage of opposites,
Magnetic intensity,
Struggle of magicians.

Knowing your internal
Place
Is a big accomplishment.

Love a lot,
Kiss a lot,
Be a lot.

The only tragedy,
Is not trusting
Angels.

The scope of Presence
Is so much larger
Than our personal vision.

Enter the pool
Of unknowing.
Shed your work boots.

To be frugal is wise,
But not when considering
The pearl of great price.

Abandon your identity,
It was only loaned anyway,
Go naked to your fate.

Great things are afforded
Those who adore
The blessed Light.

Light your candle,
Walk the path of austerity
Home.

Each love is tender and
Special;
Each of us, the same.

Both inner and outer
Silence
Can be delightful.

The Teacher says:
"They are harassing us
To birth."

How may we honor
Those who have made
The ultimate payment.

The guards at the door
Allow in
Only the pure of heart.

Don't be afraid,
All are welcome
To the feast of Love.

Call to service, privilege is
Bestowed when sufficient
Understanding is shown.

Grieving breeds
Long days
And longer nights.

Bright and fresh
The dawn of
New hope and love.

Patience is
A payment,
And a reward.

According to my friend,
Labor in the hot sun
Is Monk's work.

Sun: life-giving,
Cloud shade: relief-giving,
Each in its own way, perfect.

Timing of events
Is crucial for
Understanding meaning.

We are subject to many
Influences,
Hold fast to the lighted Way.

Philosophers think,
Scientists test, Poets dream.
Just Be.

Each moment has its own
Color, texture, drama:
Act in sync, and separate.

Baking warms houses
And spouses;
Earns kisses.

Earthbound we crave
Sky freedom,
Must grow our wings.

Lifelong learning
May provide wisdom,
Or only a packed dome.

Bow your head,
Pray for enlightenment.
Then, strap in.

We are only drops,
But so is the ocean –
Times many.

Worlds within worlds,
Applaud the diverse
Variety of amazing life.

From microbes to galaxies,
The creator
Manifests eternally.

Imaginary lines on Earth
Are human boundaries,
Not recognized by Nature.

There is a sequence
Of steps
That secures being here.

Help is given,
But often
Not comprehended.

We do not all agree,
Except on one real thing:
To Be.

Our state of being
Present,
Precludes all else.

Stumbling occurs,
Regaining footing
And ascending also.

Many hands have
Joined in the united effort
To build the Ideal State.

High impressions for
Budding souls,
Penetrate eyes and hearts.

Living well
Is a means
Not an end.

Truth, once uncovered,
Is difficult to suppress,
Bright light leaks out.

Although ignorance
Can excuse some things,
Not momentary sleep.

In the right scale
Problems
Become less significant.

Intentional conversation
Can produce
Higher understandings.

Via Higher School work,
Great friendships
Are born.

Right efforts
Are ones that bring more
Presence.

Open your inner eye
To the beauty
Of this moment.

All is material,
All is energetic,
All is here and now.

Leave your intellect
With your other tools;
Experience – as a babe.

If you are new
In each moment,
Who are you?

Discard anything
That leads you
To dreaming imagination.

If partying descends,
Choose silence and
Seclusion.

Intelligence is not
Intellect, rather a
Knowing awareness.

Few things are absolute,
Final, one hundred percent finished.
Certainly not us.

Responsibility:
Ability to respond
To the moment.

Heaven resides
In the eternal moment
Of Presence.

Deepening connection
With angels happens
When resistance ends.

Joint pool of higher awareness
Dissolves us
In divine celestial Light.

To be wise
Starts with: to be.
Wisdom may come after.

The freshness of youth
Is a reminder of
Enthusiastic optimism.

Presence, coupled with
Positive outlook and cheer,
Can open doors.

Don't underestimate
The strength of purpose
Of a tried and true heart.

Difficulties can mean
It is time to change,
Or to try harder.

Notes in music
Or steps in a sequence
Are both unique and similar.

Waking up
To seeing yourself fail,
Is a new opportunity to Be.

Each failure
Acknowledged
Is a success.

The organic process
Of soul growth
Can be confusing.

Illusions of past and future
Keep us
Immersed in identity.

While it may seem others
Have advantages,
We are all in the same boat.

The best prize life offers
Is the opportunity
To experience this moment.

Sharing lives with others
On the same journey
Is priceless.

Speaking without
Presence
Is noisy sleep.

Stay close to the
Eternal flame
Of conscious light.

Rainbow of colorful and
Intelligent students
Delights my heart.

Nothing gives as much pleasure
As being awake
To a shining moment of Love.

Don't waste time, money,
Or attention
On random temptations.

Asking for and
Receiving help,
Are very different efforts.

The light in your eyes
Helps me to light
My own.

Six moves to eternity,
Small in number,
Immense in significance.

Only Presence can
Perceive timeless
Eternity.

Students know that learning
Takes time
And patience.

Most rewards cannot
Equal efforts,
Except for Divine Presence.

A gathering of students
Foments a fountain of light
Reaching the stars.

Love for the Teacher
Ignites hearts throughout
The body ecstatic.

Emblazon your mind
With the silent light
Of heaven's immensity.

You cannot be ready
For anything,
If you are not present.

Shielding your heart
And mind against intruders
Is an ongoing struggle.

Fresh air, water, and
Impressions
Can stimulate new efforts.

We become stale
When presence
Is released.

Like a butterfly
Presence can elude
The forgetful.

Reminders are helpful
To those who
Remember to notice them.

We are not alone, ever.
Good news, except
When hiding.

So many of our illusions
Need the cover
Of darkness.

Being worldly-wise
Doesn't do much
For your level or state.

All nationalities
Are residents of Earth,
Sharing air, water, land.

A penny saved and all that,
But wrangling over pennies
Could lose you your soul.

Don't hold back,
Love with all you've got,
You will be filled again.

To estimate the value
Of something so precious,
A new scale must be invented.

Real School
Has always been,
Here.

We are all grateful
To be here,
In our School, together.

I learned about saving
When I was twelve,
I am still learning relinquishing.

Such a very great privilege
Knowing, respecting, and
Loving the best in us.

Small treasures can
Help us remember
Our true treasure.

The essence of a thing
Is more true than
Its trappings.

Graced with more than our Share,
We humbly kneel before
Angels.

We are lucky to be reminded
That we use time
For Presence.

We are each the petal
Of a very large
And fragrant Rose.

Appearances can deceive,
Inner worth is
Invisible and genuine.

Sweetness of a nubile
Soul,
Pleases tireless angels.

The game of life
Plays on,
Death is the final move.

Losing your Self in
Dreaming nonsense
Is a losing trade.

Don't gamble your
Eternal life,
For earthly ephemerals.

Wisdom does not
Preclude
Common sense.

Use your wits
To make good choices,
Not to show cleverness.

Presence is not
A pretty accessory,
But an alarming necessity.

A face graced with
Presence is beautiful,
Regardless of proportion.

Reminders for each other
In our eyes and hearts,
We are our state.

It is fortunate to be
Reflecting the strength
Of the Teacher's Love.

Our city's value
Is in its citizens,
Not in its architecture.

In the heart's core
Is recognition of true
And right action.

The way is not straight or
Smooth, but inner resolve
Promotes progress.

Vision is an incredible aid,
The Invisible
Even more so.

The arts can reflect
Higher beauty,
And lift us to new heights.

Our responsibility is
To make the most of
All the support around us.

If your dome is lighted,
Let it shine from your eyes
To all in your view.

Opposite extremes
Are runaway queens,
Handle gently.

Finding answers is not
Nearly as important
As being them.

Deliberation extended
Can falsely masquerade
As deep thought.

Quiet your mind,
Open your heart,
Be where you are.

The road may be difficult;
Ascending, however,
Is the only way to go.

Carry love and light
With you on your journey
To the stars.

Fame in sleeping minds
Is worthless
In eternity.

Valuing the right things
Makes your worth
Escalate.

Partners in life's journey
Can assist lessons
Necessary to evolve.

Our likes, loves, and
Marriages
Are spiritually arranged.

We are instrumental
To each other's
Development.

How fortunate that our tiny
Will can be directed
To Be.

Old ideas that helped us
Recognize truth
Are dissolved in the Light.

It is beyond lucky
To have a play with
Purpose.

Disaster is a life
Wasted
In sleep.

Records are kept
To ensure
Mistakes are not repeated.

Even mistakes can
Facilitate
New being.

There is no objective
History,
Without being in Presence.

When climbing to the light
Remove
The blinders.

Smooth sailing imagination
Feels real,
Without Light.

Sensing the condition
Of body and emotions,
Gives illusion of being.

Shed illusions.
Reality can open
To Third Eye.

The challenge of
Being present to life
Is daily Olympics.

Awake and present,
We become
Our Selves.

Small and slow developing,
With many hurdles to pass,
We continue by grace.

Intense emotions
Move like lightning
Only presence can catch.

To prepare for the day,
Include patience
With the tools in your pack.

Letting go of old desires
Takes frank examining,
Presence and open heart.

Being full of light,
Many fears and accounts
Fall away for lack of room.

A clear-lighted nothing
Is the success of good
House cleaning.

Moon and Sun are both full,
Energies radiating
Through the solar system.

Cosmic influences
Move our limbs and hearts;
We watch and learn.

Sequential steps to
Freedom
Need only pure presence.

If you think carefully,
Conclude:
No alternative to effort.

To find inner resolve,
Seek deep understandings
Via previous verifications.

Friends can give
Thoughtful alternatives
To our stuck opinions.

Kindness and harmony
Are hallmarks of a
Light-filled being.

Extend your hand to those
Who need
More light.

Seeing an action
Beneath your standards;
Don't judge, repent.

Love inside and out,
We are swimming in the
Shining sea.

Obeying the Gods
Seems confusing;
A lifelong challenge.

Floating above the Earth
With a thousand questions;
First: Who am I?

Second: Why am I here?
Third: Is this all there is?
Fourth: How can I serve?

Being serves
Better
Than knowing.

Peel back the onion layers,
Find the inmost meaning,
Enigma foiled.

Life is a payment,
Be careful of your
Purchase.

It does not matter which
Road you take,
If you have no destination.

Actions convince
Better than words,
But words can help.

A whole vineyard of grapes
Unfermented
Cannot fill a single cup.

Laugh at yourself,
Better than lament;
Never laugh at the Gods.

Feeling weighed down.
Time to remember:
Only necessity is Presence.

To think outside the box,
You must first
See the box.

It's a lot of pressure
To be the center
Of the Universe.

The enemy of my aim
Is usually
Me.

Weariness of heart
Needs refreshing from
Light and love.

Patience, perseverance,
And a plethora of help
Is needed to evolve.

The more malleable,
The easier to affect;
Hard as rock, difficult.

Mother and Father
Earth and Heaven
Temporal and Eternal.

Caught in the middle
Of colossal opposites,
We have our little life.

Don't decorate your prison.
Find a way out,
Now.

Sometimes we only realize
Our Selves through
Others.

Being particular is useful,
But sticking to minutiae
Can reduce meaning.

Loving others
Helps us
Love our Selves.

The world can seem cruel.
Workings of Gods is a
Mystery we can't solve.

It is never foolish
To spend your life
Living in the present.

Desert to mountaintop,
Earth's biosphere
Nourishes land beings.

Our shining blue oceans
Are full of rubbish
We are guilty of neglecting.

Make certain of not
Neglecting
Your Self.

How little we accord
Simple gratitude
To Nature's plenty.

Moment to moment,
Proceed
With humility.

Reward
And effort
Are one.

Dedicate your inner world
To the shining light of
Presence.

Lavish your praise
On deserving
Angels.

Some of the best
Things are invisible:
Angels, Love, Presence.

To serve means:
Knowing how to
Not obstruct higher will.

Grace in appearance
Can never exceed
True internal grace.

Love for the innocent
Is remembering
Home.

Hook your desire
To the love
Of Presence.

A quiet environment
Can facilitate a
Spacious, quiet mind.

A growing light in the
Quiet dark can lead to
Wondrous enlightenment.

Be.
A monosyllable of
Great portent.

To reflect
The divine light
Is a great honor.

The long upward path of
Evolution
Has led to this very instant.

One perceives beauty
Because it circulates
Within.

See beauty everywhere
And be full of beauty:
Beautiful!

People don't discriminate
Against black or white
Dogs.

When anger flares
Remember
Who you really are.

Presence can defuse
Most petty
Grievances.

Hurt vanity
Does not need
To heal.

Celebrate your luck
With copious
Gratitude.

Dear friends
Can save us
From wasting in self-pity.

Although sleep
Is a piteous state,
Self-pity will descend lower.

There is no cure
For a rebellious
Soul.

You are what you eat,
What you think,
What you do.

When cleaning your house,
Clean your inner house
At the same time.

Opportunities persist,
Don't resist,
Insist on presence.

Having trouble?
Six steps to
Solution.

The Earth's tilt has landed on
Summer once again,
Sun's anchoring gift.

We are creatures
Of heaven and earth
And partake of both.

Lemon meringue pie
Cooling on counter,
Fragrant sustenance.

Sometimes life is simple,
But never satisfying
Without presence.

So many impressions,
Color, depth, variety;
Only one still space.

We are the genuine article,
The real deal,
When we are truly present.

Mid-Summer Madness,
Solstice – a crack
In the austere facade.

Different strengths and talents are gifted
By Heaven's Muse;
Comply.

The struggle to be awake
To our lives
Is more than our struggle.

We have had help
From the very beginning,
Invisible guidance.

We need our tools
Handy and available
To stay in this moment.

Turn your face to the flame,
Warm your allegiance
With your devotion.

Our plans often don't work,
As they are subject to
Divine intervention.

If you feel confused,
It is a chance to
Reprioritize.

A positive outlook
Is not naiveté,
Rather a choice of optimism.

Increment by increment
We grow into
Our Selves.

Time, the grand illusion,
Useful for seizing
This moment.

A baby quickly learns
The laws of this world,
Unlearning is a lifetime.

Many things to remember,
The main thing
Is your Self.

Peering out the window
I see my reflection;
In and out simultaneously.

Attention divided
Is attention
Spent and saved.

Beginnings can be difficult,
The smallest shift
Can connect to Be.

Just actually seeing
Your surroundings
Is a good start.

Take up the challenge,
Commit yourself
To experiencing your life.

Our bodies, minds, feelings,
Intermingle with
Life's complications.

It is best to stay
Simple and focused,
The present moment is all.

God-realization is as near
As the release of all
Illusions.

Being precise, or correct,
Is not nearly as important
As being Present.

Even at a lower level
Love is useful.
Highest love is God.

The alchemy of
Transformation,
Is truly a miracle:

Tapping the energy
Of negative emotions
To raise one's state.

Being present connects
To possibilities
Usually inaccessible.

Our state of being fluctuates
Momentarily,
Until crystallizing correctly.

Love opens the way
To receive blessings
From the angels.

Presence is our blessing
And our gift
Of reciprocal gratitude.

We transcend our mind,
Heart, and body,
Entering the timeless state.

Death: The transition
From bodily experience
To energy re-formed.

Fearing death is fearing life,
Both are unfathomable
And inevitable.

Some things can only be
Understood
By shifting scale.

Time is relinquished
Along with other illusions,
In Eternity.

Accepting what comes
With grace and love
Is a very high state.

Abandon grievances and
All feelings of disrespect;
Shift to gratitude and love.

Anger, irritation, feels real;
It is not real, but a reaction
From an unrealized being.

The Muses confer together
To drop their magic onto
A chosen lucky artist.

All benefit from the labor
Of master artists,
Talent gifted from above.

The music of the spheres
Is a cosmic vibration
With which we resonate.

Thoughtfulness is not
Forgotten
By the universe.

Good karma is earned.
Choose carefully
Daily activities.

The grand design
Is a hothouse of
Life recycling.

If there were aliens, they
Would have to comply
With laws, like the rest of us.

It is not the number of eyes
That you have, but if you can
Truly see through them.

Animals are aware,
But not present;
A requirement of evolution.

It is a trick of life on earth,
That we know the past,
But not the future.

The future does not exist, ever;
Only the present moment exists:
Join it.

The Angel of Death calls
We know not when;
Our chance to live is now.

The ascending pathway
May be more difficult,
But it's the only way to go.

Love the present moment
With all you've got.
It is all there is.

Great and small
Things of the Earth
Eat and are eaten.

You would not eat poison,
Or breathe it;
Don't view it either.

It is very fortunate to be able
To discern the various levels
Of impressions.

Don't waste time,
Money, or energy
On trivial distractions.

We are grateful for much.
Luckily, we can repay
With presence.

Remove old attitudes
With your scrub brush,
Be a good householder.

This, our gestation,
May seem strange;
How incredible, rebirth.

We are baby angels;
We must be watched,
Guided, chastised.

Training isn't always fun;
A necessity,
Understood in retrospect.

Lift your face to the Sun,
Say your prayers
With joy in your heart.

Another day of
Friendship,
Love, and good will.

Patiently waiting
Is an active effort,
Not a passive giving up.

The timing of the angels
Is very different
From our schedule.

At times,
Verifications
Need refreshing.

All you know,
You have known before
And will know again.

The mirror will not
Tell you
Who you really are.

Aging is a signal that
Transition from this
Current body is near.

Nothing is lost,
Recycling
Continues.

Be not alarmed,
Love fortifies
All growing souls.

An instant is enough time
To perceive
Truth.

Listen carefully to the
Uplifting melody,
A reminder of true home.

Be: the beginning
And ending of the same
Lightning charge.

Leaving solid ground
Is not an easy decision,
Every bird has to do it.

In order to fly
One must
Lighten the load.

Raise the sails,
The good wind
Will push us home.

Love the journey
As much as you can,
It is uniquely yours.

Our role to play may seem
Small and insignificant;
The Play requires all parts.

Madness in life
Can make us feel sane,
But how sane is sleep?

Drifting in the sea
Of imagination
Is madness.

We alert each other
To stay awake to
The ever-present moment.

A slow and methodical
Path to the present,
Accomplished in six steps.

Each particular view
Contributes to the sphere
Of full understanding.

Try to not shoot the
Messenger
Who wakes You.

All is relative
Except the one thing,
This present moment.

Longing for space-time to
Breathe, stretch and feel
The salty sea breeze.

We need all the help
Provided to us,
Sleep is the default.

Is it really You who
Eats your food,
Makes your decisions?

Marriage can teach
Trust and unselfish love,
If presence is practiced.

Duality rules this level
Of existence,
Only transcended by Love.

To develop will
Stop thoughts,
Be in every moment.

Be on the crown to decide
Between conserving and
Spending energy.

In order to be united,
Presence must preside
Over all decisions.

Valuation for our blessings
Makes an opening
For higher influences.

True governing
Comes from realizing
One's position.

The generous outpouring
Of conscious Love
Is our medium of thriving.

Mothers have to protect and
Teach their children,
And separate from results.

Many students have
Specialized talents,
All designed to serve.

Invisible milestones;
Silently acknowledge
Ascent on the path.

Earth's development seems
Eternal;
Just a different time scale.

Nature works with fine matter
And forces
Invisible to our eyes.

Angels know our difficulties,
Been there,
Done that.

Pleading with angels,
Fruitless,
They know their allegiance.

Luckily,
We can be timeless
Users of time.

Retracing conclusions,
Finding assumptions,
Prejudices, and falsehoods.

Without the
Light of Presence
We are truly blind.

Angels could be justified
In frustration with us,
But bear with patience.

Clean sheets, a cup of tea,
A smile. Sometimes it is all
Very simple.

Occasionally there occurs
An unexpected incident;
Planned, but not by us.

The only way to be prepared
For anything
Is to be present.

A glass of wine, a special book,
A quiet evening;
A haven.

Meaning is not in life,
But within
Each of us.

Giving what is needed
Is better than
Giving what is wanted.

Love is
The means
And the destination.

Hearts united in presence
Is a marriage
Made in Heaven.

Surrendering to
The highest influence,
Is a win-win.

Random thoughts
Can disturb, or worse,
Capture mind and heart.

Protect your Self
With presence
And intentionality.

Hopefully we are the
Kings, not the Jacks,
Of all trades.

A magnificent Light Sphere
Graciously descends
To enlighten our hearts.

Uncreated Light
Illuminates those who
See clearly in its radiance.

Whoever you are,
Wherever you are,
Accept your play with Gratitude.

To enlist the aid
Of an avenging angel,
Wage war against the foe.

Never underestimate
The unscrupulous
Behavior of lower mind.

Look no further for the foe
Than just below
Your navel.

He grumbles,
Complains,
And is generally unhappy.

Worst of all,
He tells stories
Of your lack of worth.

Truth cannot be reached
Without right efforts, and
Presence to light the way.

For some,
Higher School
Is a reality.

Soft flutter of angel's wings
Can open
Ear of your heart.

Earth's colors are vivid,
But not as bright
As Heaven's hues.

Take special care of all
Windows into this world
That we share.

Eyes, ears, minds, hearts
Perceive, but can deceive
A budding soul.

Duality misleads a deeper
Understanding
Of invisible forces acting.

"Stop!" – can help thwart
Intrusions into inner life.
Watch, you are watched.

Actions have reactions,
Only the third force
Can resolve dichotomy.

Movement is necessity,
But does not denote
Life, or Reality.

We were taught to share and
Play fair, despite our
Selfish youth.

There may not be fairness,
But there may be higher
Justice, ultimately.

The universe's long life
May only be a movie to
Entertain unknowables.

There are no bounds on
Imagination,
Ask Hollywood.

When times are more
Difficult,
We become more certain.

We are surprised by events
Because we cannot see
Currents beyond our sight.

No matter how many
Combinations are made,
Basic elements are needed.

The Gods designed us
To be like them, even so
We are a work in progress.

Little Wisdoms

A finished man exceeds
Our expectations, as the
Sun outshines the moon.

What color is water? Air?
We reflect
What does not belong to us.

The top of the mountain
Is not enough,
We must persist, go higher.

Runaway queens
Can cause havoc,
Rein in the horses with love.

The best gift given is
Presence, and better yet,
Received with presence.

Speak little,
Listen a lot,
See everything.

The purpose of money
Is to be circulated,
Not hoarded.

Sometimes the thing
Most needed eludes us,
Intensifying our valuation.

When our spiritual needs
Outweigh bodily ones,
The doorway opens.

A fragrant garden
Affords sensual delight,
Used for presence: Bliss.

Take aim,
The target is in sight,
Your own higher Self.

Heaven may celebrate
When we finally are able
To make right efforts.

Our lives seem long,
But length is not important
As amount of presence.

To reflect the light of
Heaven,
Become an empty mirror.

Angels working on our behalf
Carry weapons
And healing balm.

Fears that hold us back
Can be dropped;
Realizing their unreality.

Fellow travelers on
The evolutionary path
Can assist our progress.

It is impossible to evaluate
Our priceless
Friendships.

Although we are ordinary,
Correct valuation
Is extraordinary.

The knife's edge
Is sleep or awakening,
To be or not to be.

Many symbols guide us;
When we are present,
We rise past needing them.

To unlock potential,
Use the key of presence,
And the eye of the crown.

When the force of Love
Swirls through your heart,
Kneel and bless your luck.

Shimmering and white,
Light from above
Reveals all perfectly.

Little Wisdoms

Angels do not need
To speak to communicate
Their guidance.

Controlling our speech
Can show much about
Our inner motives.

Conflicting desires
Confuse, disturb, and
Compromise our aims.

With the right
Governing factor in place,
Functions align beneath.

Remembering to Be,
Can start the progress
Of flight to the stars.

Self-accepted restrictions,
And a lot of help,
Can create real freedom.

Nothing is more dangerous
Than the illusion
Of safety.

Humanity is mortal,
Each one of us
Is temporary.

Only that which is invisible,
Intangible, and unimagined
Can be immortal.

The river of change
Cannot sweep away
The stillness of presence.

Forces in opposition
To one's aim
Can be traction needed.

Students of the Teacher
Of consciousness
Labor within themselves.

Tracing our movements
Through space and time,
Dynamic patterns appear.

Out of time,
The kaleidoscope
Of one student is precious.

Blessed hierarchy of God,
Angels, enlightened teachers,
And students.

The pyramid of Love,
Pierces space to
Touch the gates of Heaven.

The Greeks envisioned
Golden cities of truth and
Justice, a noble pursuit.

Each citizen must have
Presence circulating,
For this accomplishment.

What is fated is often
Difficult to discern,
Yet is revealed in time.

Uncreated Light
Makes the Impossible,
Possible.

Let your beauty be
Presence crowning
Your dome of light.

Sincere smiles
Make faces beautiful,
Especially present ones.

Simple isn't always easy,
Complex isn't better,
There's no formula for truth.

Treasures of the Earth
Have no comparison
To Heaven's treasure.

Let your treasure reside
In the sacred room
Of your loving heart.

Finally, when all is said and done,
Seeing yourself see,
Is enough.

www.ingramcontent.com/pod-product-compliance
Lightning Source LLC
Chambersburg PA
CBHW031416290426
44110CB00011B/398